# Teaching Little Fingers to Play
# Ukulele

## Lessons for the Earliest Beginner
### By Michael Ezra

Illustrations by Nick Gressle

ISBN 978-1-5400-3052-8

WILLIS MUSIC

EXCLUSIVELY DISTRIBUTED BY

HAL•LEONARD®

**PLAYBACK+**
Speed • Pitch • Balance • Loop

To access audio, visit:
**www.halleonard.com/mylibrary**

Enter Code
3705-6853-0106-3516

Visit Hal Leonard Online at
**www.halleonard.com**

Contact us:
**Hal Leonard**
7777 West Bluemound Road
Milwaukee, WI 53213
Email: info@halleonard.com

In Europe, contact:
**Hal Leonard Europe Limited**
42 Wigmore Street
Marylebone, London, W1U 2RN
Email: info@halleonardeurope.com

In Australia, contact:
**Hal Leonard Australia Pty. Ltd.**
4 Lentara Court
Cheltenham, Victoria, 3192 Australia
Email: info@halleonard.com.au

# FOR PARENTS & GUARDIANS

This is your child's first ukulele book. Since the ukulele is a small instrument, it is well-suited for a child's small hands. If you will assist the teacher by arousing your child's interest and enthusiasm in each successive lesson, the result will speak for itself.

Lyrics have been added to the music examples to help interpret the spirit of the little songs. Read them with your child and explain their meaning. These songs were carefully written to be both simple and fun. Help your child keep a steady beat while strumming.

The online audio tracks will speed up the learning process and build confidence as your child practices at home. Don't be afraid to get involved and sing along!

Encourage your child as he/she learns new musical skills. You might even be inspired to learn a new instrument yourself!

# FOR TEACHERS
## How to Present the First Two Lessons

### Lesson 1

1. Begin the first lesson by introducing the child to the ukulele, naming its parts and inviting him/her to touch and explore the instrument.

2. Take a few moments to tune strings 4, 3 and 2. After observing the procedure, let the child try to tune string 1.

3. Demonstrate the proper way to hold the instrument and explain how fingers are numbered on the fret hand.

4. While teaching the C chord, demonstrate proper fret-hand and strumming technique.

5. Play and sing the first song (using all downstrums) and have the child imitate you.

### Lesson 2

1. Explain how chord diagrams work, demonstrating with the C chord and the new F chord.

2. Introduce the concepts of measures and bar lines.

3. Demonstrate with the song "Back and Forth."

4. Explain note values and how to count beats.

5. Demonstrate with the song "Birthday Party."

# LESSON 1
## PARTS OF THE UKULELE

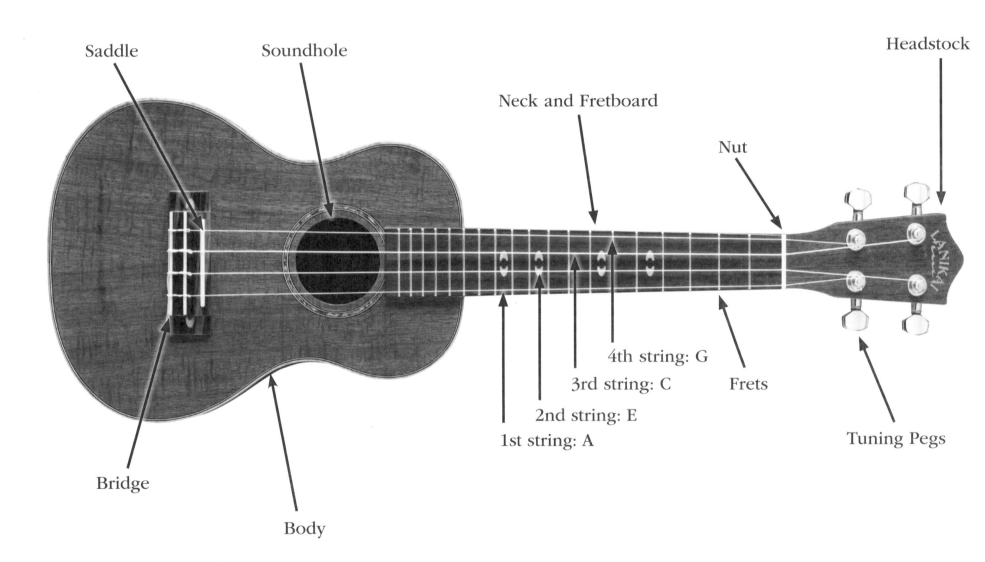

Saddle

Soundhole

Neck and Fretboard

Headstock

Nut

4th string: G

3rd string: C

Frets

2nd string: E

1st string: A

Tuning Pegs

Bridge

Body

# HOLDING THE UKULELE

There are many ways to hold a ukulele, both sitting and standing.

### Sitting

- Sit up straight and relax your shoulders

- Place your feet flat on the floor or place one foot on a foot stool

- Tilt the neck of the ukulele slightly upwards

- Rest the ukulele on your leg or keep it in place by cradling it with your arm against your body

### Standing

- Cradle the ukulele under the strumming arm to keep it in place

- Don't squeeze too tightly

- Tilt the neck of the ukulele slightly upwards

### Wearing a Strap

Alternatively, you can wear a strap to keep your ukulele in place (sitting or standing). This will also allow the instrument to vibrate more freely and generally produce a bigger sound.

# PLAYING THE UKULELE

You can strum the strings with your thumb or index finger. Most people strum where the neck meets the body.

Your fret hand is used to play notes on the neck. The fingers are numbered 1–4.

When fretting notes, keep your fingers curved and use your fingertips to press the string just behind the fret. Don't let your knuckles bend backward.

# C CHORD

It's time to learn your first chord! This is called a C major chord, and you only need one finger to play it.

Place your third finger on fret 3 of string 1 and strum all the strings from top to bottom. Once you get the hang of it, try playing this song. The rhythm slashes **/** tell you when to strum, and the chord symbol above tells you which chord to play. For this song, just strum the C chord with a steady beat.

## Strum the Ukulele

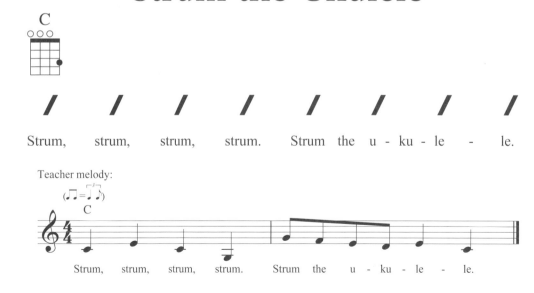

C

/ / / / / / / /

Strum,     strum,     strum,     strum.     Strum the u - ku - le - le.

Teacher melody:

C

Strum,     strum,     strum,     strum.     Strum the u - ku - le - le.

# LESSON 2

A **chord diagram** is an easy way to show how a chord is played on the ukulele. The vertical (up and down) lines represent the strings, and the horizontal (side to side) lines represent the frets. Dots on the frets show where to put your fingers. A zero (0) above a string tells you to play that string "open," without pressing any frets. The numbers inside the circles tell you which fingers to use.

Here's what the C chord looks like on a diagram:

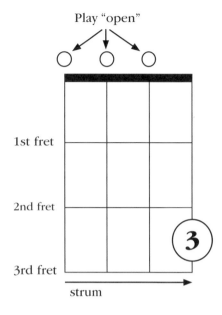

Play "open"

1st fret

2nd fret

3rd fret

3

strum

## F Chord

Let's learn another chord! This one is called F major, and here's the diagram:

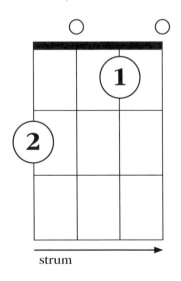

1

2

strum

Music is divided into **measures** using **bar lines**. This makes it easier to keep your place.
(Imagine reading a book that had no punctuation!)
A **double bar line** is used at the end of a piece of music.

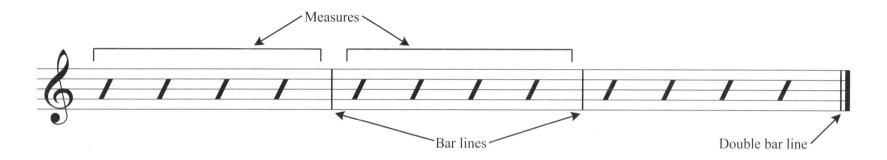

Let's try using C and F chords in a song that uses measures and bar lines.

# Back and Forth

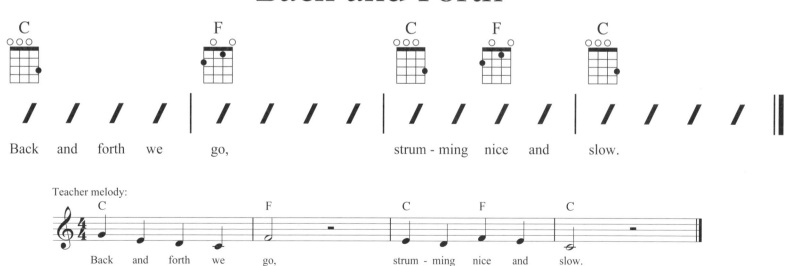

Back    and    forth    we    go,                    strum - ming    nice    and    slow.

Teacher melody:

Back    and    forth    we    go,                    strum - ming    nice    and    slow.

# RHYTHM

In music, we can count the beats to keep our place in the music. This is called **rhythm**.

Just like money coins, different notes have different rhythmic values:

A **quarter note** is held for 1 beat

A **half note** is held for 2 beats

A **whole note** is held for 4 beats

In rhythm slashes, these notes look like this:

Quarter note

Half note

Whole note

Here's a song to try some rhythms with our C and F chords.

## Birthday Party

Huff   and   puff,         blow   and   blow.         Out   the   birth - day   can - dles   go!

Count:   1      2      3    (4)     1      2      3    (4)     1      2      3      4      1      2      3    (4)

Teacher melody:

Huff   and   puff,     blow   and   blow.     Out   the   birth - day   can - dles   go!

# LESSON 3

A **time signature** tells us how a song should be counted.

**4/4** Top number tells us there are four beats in a measure
Bottom number tells us that each quarter note gets one beat

**3/4** Top number tells us there are three beats in a measure
Bottom number tells us that each quarter note gets one beat

## Bedtime

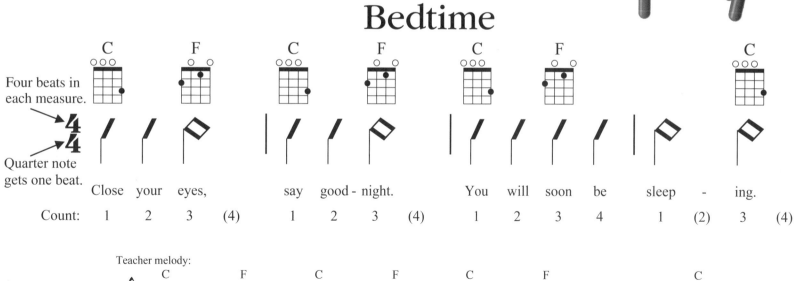

# A MINOR CHORD

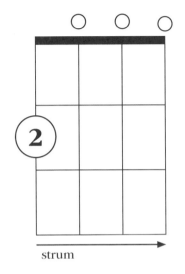

strum

Major chords sound happy, while minor chords sound sad. Let's learn your first minor chord: A minor. The symbol for this chord is **Am**.

# Rain on the Roof

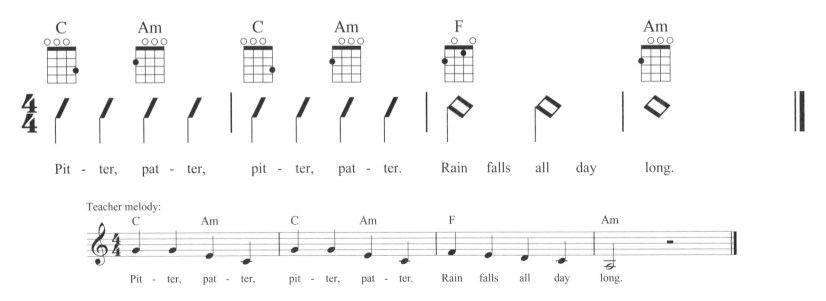

Pit - ter, pat - ter, pit - ter, pat - ter. Rain falls all day long.

Teacher melody:

Pit - ter, pat - ter, pit - ter, pat - ter. Rain falls all day long.

Hint: While you're playing one chord, you can sometimes get your other fingers ready for the next chord. Since you're using your third finger for the C chord, you can get your second finger ready for the Am chord!

# G CHORD

To play a G major chord, we need three fingers. It makes a little triangle shape on the ukulele neck.

A time signature of $\frac{3}{4}$ means there are three beats in each measure, and the quarter note gets one beat. A **dot** increases a note's value by half. So, the final strum—the dotted half note—should be held for three beats.

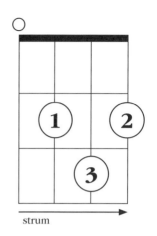

strum

# Baseball Days

Three beats in each measure.

Quarter note gets one beat.

You grab the glove.    I'll grab the ball.

Meet at the field.    Come one and all.

Teacher melody:

You grab the glove. ___    I'll grab the ball. ___    Meet at the field. ___    Come one and all.

# LESSON 4

We don't have to strum every song with the same rhythm—
that would be boring! In the next song, the strum pattern is basically
the opposite of what we used in "Bedtime" (page 11).

## Trip to the Mailbox

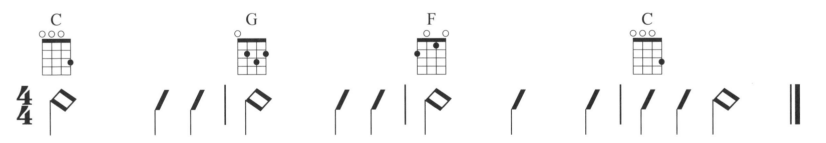

Let-ters in the mail,     wait-ing for   me.     How man-y are there? Count:   one,  two,  three.

Teacher melody:

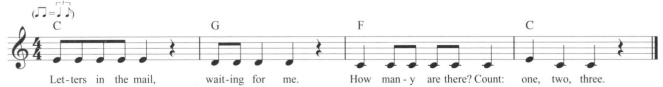

Let-ters in the mail,     wait-ing for   me.     How man-y are there? Count:   one,  two,  three.

# D MINOR CHORD

Let's learn another minor chord.
This one is called D minor, or Dm.

A **rest** tells you to be silent. Just as there are different note values, there are also different rest values:

Quarter-note rest

(Silent 1 beat)

Half-note rest

(Silent 2 beats)

Whole-note rest

(Silent 4 beats)

Use the palm of your strumming hand to quiet the strings during the rests.

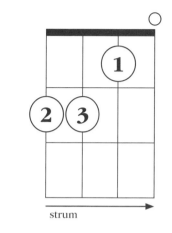

strum

# Superhero Song

Am | Dm

May-be I will be a su-per-he-ro, fight-ing crime all day long. I

Am | C G Am

know I'll be a per-fect su-per-he-ro. I've al-read-y got my su-per-he-ro song.

Teacher melody:

Am | Dm

May-be I will be a su-per-he-ro, fight-ing crime all day long. I

Am | C G Am

know I'll be a per-fect su-per-he-ro. I've al-read-y got my su-per-he-ro song.

Let's try a different strum pattern with rests. In the previous song,
we were strumming on beats 1 and 3 and resting on beats 2 and 4. Now we'll reverse that.

The curved line ⌒ connecting the last two notes is called a **tie**.
This combines the rhythm of two notes into one. When you play the last C chord on beat 4,
hold it (let it ring) all the way through the whole note in the next measure.

# Frogs in a Bog

Strum - min' down the riv - er, lis - t'nin' to the frogs.

"Croak, croak, croak," so hap-py in their bog.

Teacher melody:

Strum - min' down the riv - er, lis - t'nin' to the frogs.

"Croak, croak, croak," so hap-py in their bog.

# LESSON 5
## D CHORD

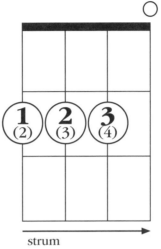

strum

This chord might feel a little cramped because you have to put three fingers on the same fret. Notice that there are two fingering choices—try both to see which one feels better.

Sometimes one fingering is easier depending on the other chords you're playing, as you'll see later.

# EIGHTH NOTES

The value of an **eighth note** is half as long as a quarter note. We can play two eighth notes in one beat, counting like this: "1 & 2 & 3 & 4 &."

To play eighth notes, you'll strum both down ↓ and up ↑. Strum up between the beats, as you count "&."

Let's practice strumming eighth notes using your brand-new D chord. To help you know which way to strum, arrows have been added over the eighth notes.

## Off to the Races

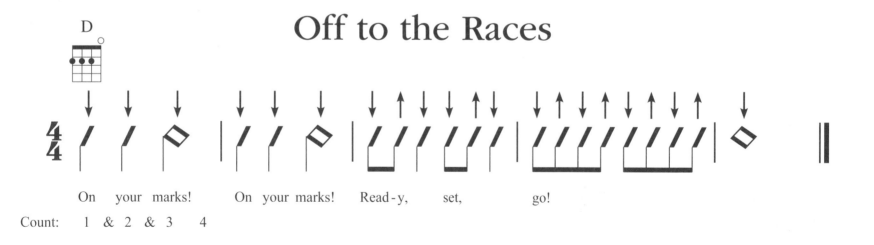

Let's keep practicing eighth notes using the two minor chords you've learned so far. Don't forget to count!

# Song of the Volga Boatmen

Music can be written in happy keys (major) and sad keys (minor). This famous Russian folk melody is written in a sad key. Many years ago, before there were steamboats, peasants who lived near the Volga River had to physically pull boats and barges loaded with merchandise up the river from one village to the next. While struggling with their heavy loads, they would sing this song to help pass the time.

# LESSON 6
## A CHORD

The A major chord is nice and easy—you only need two fingers!

You'll switch between A major and D major chords in this song. Look back at the two possible D chord fingerings on page 17. In this case, the 2-3-4 fingering is easier because you can leave your middle finger in the same spot (fret 2, string 4) throughout the whole song!

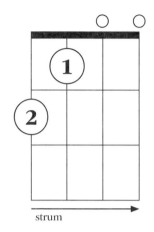

strum

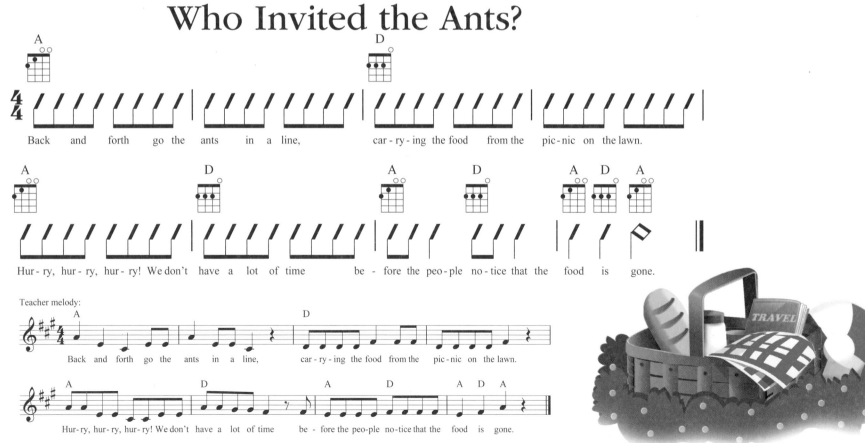

# Who Invited the Ants?

A

D

$\frac{4}{4}$ / / / / / / / | / / / / / / / | / / / / / / / | / / / / / / / |

Back  and  forth  go the  ants  in a  line,  car-ry-ing the food  from the  pic-nic on the lawn.

A          D          A          D          A  D  A

/ / / / / / / | / / / / / / / | / / / / | / / / ◇ ‖

Hur-ry, hur-ry, hur-ry! We don't have a  lot  of  time  be-fore the peo-ple no-tice that the  food  is  gone.

Teacher melody:

A                    D

Back and forth go the  ants  in a  line,  car-ry-ing the food  from the  pic-nic on the lawn.

A          D          A    D    A D A

Hur-ry, hur-ry, hur-ry! We don't have a  lot  of  time  be-fore the peo-ple no-tice that the  food  is  gone.

# SHUFFLE FEEL

So far we've been playing eighth notes evenly, so they're all the same length. But it's very common to use a **shuffle feel** for the eighth notes. This creates a lopsided sound where the first eighth note in each beat is longer than the second. The popular children's song "Itsy Bitsy Spider" is sung this way.

The symbol for a shuffle feel is ( ♫ = ♩♪ ). When you see that at the beginning of a song, it's supposed to be played with a shuffle feel. Sometimes you may just see the words "Shuffle feel" or "Swing feel," and those mean the same thing.

Let's try it out now!

## The Hammock Song

# C7 CHORD

The C7 chord is very similar to the C chord, but it's played on fret 1 instead of fret 3. Try switching between C and C7 several times to hear the difference.

Once you get the hang of C7, let's try it in a song.

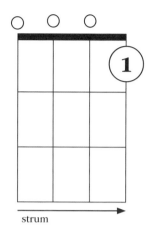

strum

# Grandma's Cookies

# LESSON 7
## B♭ CHORD

B♭ major (read as "B-flat") is a type of **barre chord**. This means that you'll lay one finger flat across two or more strings at the same fret. In the case of B♭, your first finger presses strings 1 and 2 at the first fret.

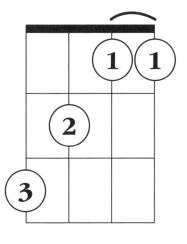

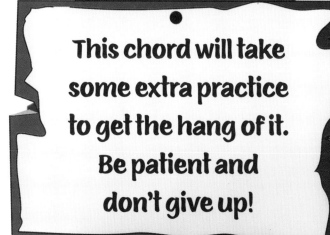

This chord will take some extra practice to get the hang of it. Be patient and don't give up!

24

Here's a song that uses your new C7 and B♭ chords. You may have heard it sung during the Christmas season.

# Good King Wenceslas

For the next song, we're playing with a shuffle feel in ¾.
The rhythm should be counted "1, 2 & 3 &."

# The Spider Web

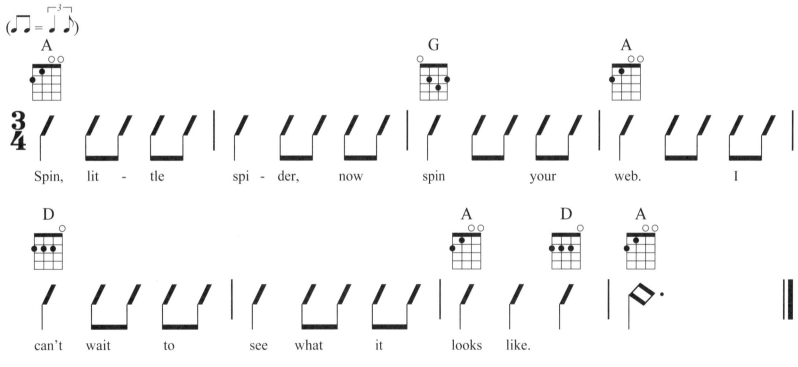

Spin,   lit – tle   spi – der,   now   spin   your   web.   I

can't   wait   to   see   what   it   looks   like.

Teacher melody:

Spin, lit – tle spi – der, now   spin   your   web.   I   can't wait to   see what it   looks like.

# LESSON 8
## G7 CHORD

G7 is similar to the G major chord, but the little triangle shape points the other way.

Before trying the next song, look at the next-to-last measure. The dots over the slashes are called **staccato**, which means they should be played in a short, clipped manner. So, instead of letting those strums ring for a full quarter note, immediately stop the sound with the palm of your strumming hand.

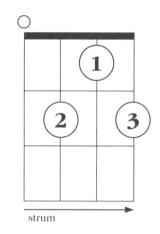

strum

# Flying to the Moon

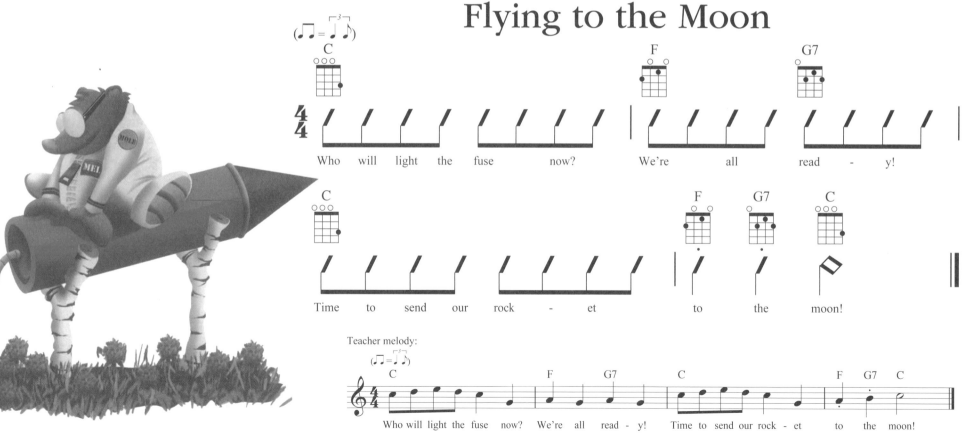

We're mixing more staccato notes into our strumming pattern in this next song.

# The Hill

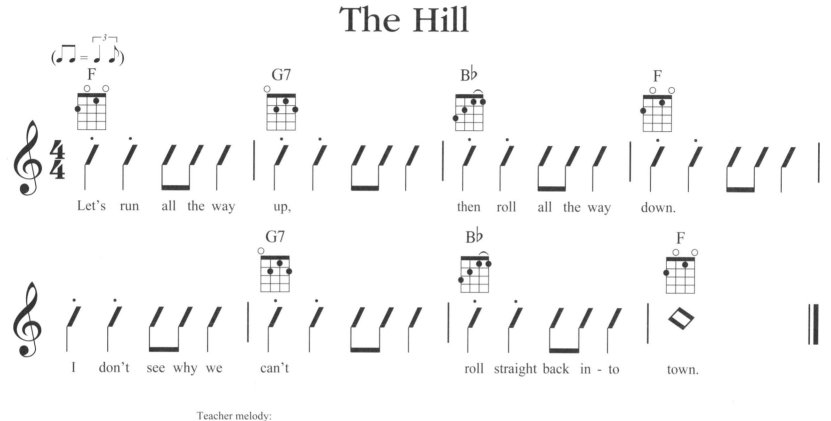

Let's run    all    the   way    up,        then  roll   all   the  way    down.

I    don't   see   why   we    can't        roll  straight  back  in - to     town.

Teacher melody:

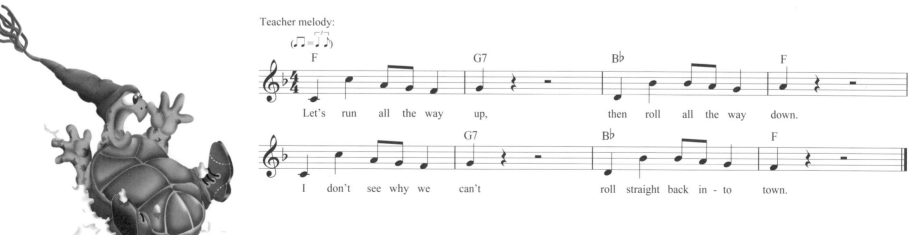

Let's  run   all   the  way    up,       then  roll   all   the   way   down.

I    don't   see   why  we    can't       roll  straight back  in - to    town.

# D7 CHORD

The D7 chord is super easy! Start with a
D major chord, but play string 3 open.

strum

# By the Pond

G                    C

**4/4**

"Rib - bit,   rib - bit,   rib - bit,"   cries   the   frog   up - on   the   rock.

D7                  G      D7      G

"Don't   you   mean   quack?"   says   the   duck   up - on   the   dock.

Teacher melody:

(♫ = ♪♪)

G                    C

"Rib - bit,   rib - bit,   rib - bit,"   cries   the   frog   up - on   the   rock.

D7               G      D7      G

"Don't   you   mean   quack?"   says   the   duck   up - on   the   dock.

# LESSON 9

In the next song, we're accenting certain counts by strumming a bit harder. The accents fall on beats 2 and 4, and they're marked in the music with the > symbol.

## Cricket in a Hurry

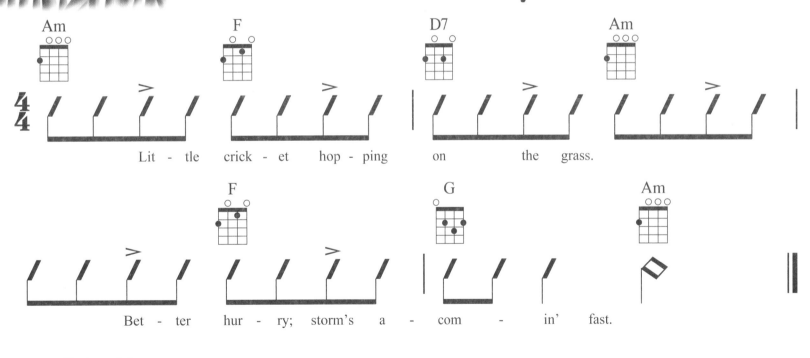

Lit - tle crick - et hop - ping on the grass.

Bet - ter hur - ry; storm's a - com - in' fast.

Teacher melody:

Lit - tle crick-et hop-ping on the grass. _____ Bet-ter hur - ry; storm's a - com - in' fast. _____

# A7 CHORD

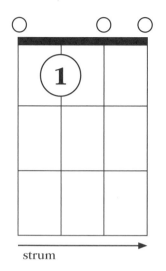

strum

To play A7, start with an A major chord, but play string 4 open.

Now that you've learned D7, G7 and A7, you can play a cool blues song for your final piece!

Watch the strum patterns closely— there are two different ones.

# Walkin' Shoes Blues

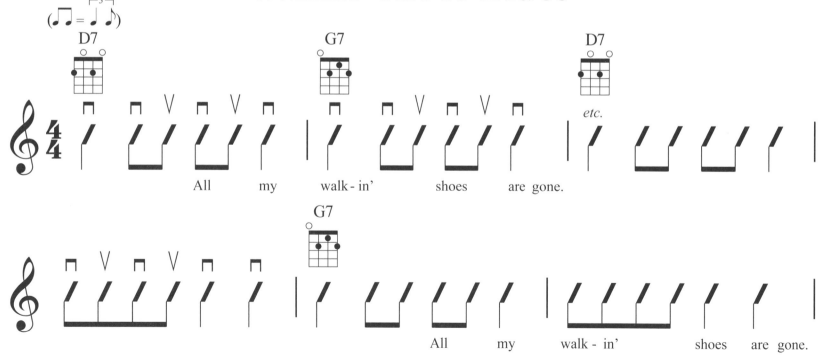

Now I'm walk-in' on my

bare feet all day long.

Teacher melody:

All my walk-in' shoes are gone. ___

All my walk-in' shoes are gone. ___

Now I'm walk-in' on my bare feet all day long. ___

# CERTIFICATE of MERIT

This certifies that

...................................................................................................................

has successfully completed

## TEACHING LITTLE FINGERS TO PLAY
### UKULELE

.....................................................................

*Teacher*

.....................................................................

*Date*